# Visual Impact

## The Ultimate Guide to Website and Social Media Graphics



Cover Design By Frank E. Deardurff II



**Disclaimer**

The information contained in this book is for educational and informational purposes only. Every effort has been made to ensure that the content provided is accurate and helpful for small business owners and entrepreneurs. However, the author makes no representations or warranties of any kind, express or implied, about the completeness, accuracy, reliability, or suitability of the advice provided. The results you achieve from implementing the strategies or tips shared in this book may vary and depend on many factors, including but not limited to your market, industry, website, and marketing efforts.

This book is not intended to provide professional, legal, or technical advice. Readers should consult with a professional advisor for their unique situation before making any changes to their business or website. The author assumes no responsibility for errors or omissions, or for any damages resulting from the use of the information contained in this book.

# Table of Contents

    - Consequences of stretching, cropping, and improper dimensions.
    - Quick reference guide for the latest dimensions across major social platforms.
- **Chapter 4: Brand Consistency in Visuals**
    - Why maintaining brand consistency builds trust and recognition.
    - Developing a visual style guide for graphics: colors, filters, and effects.
    - Real-world examples of brands that use visuals effectively for consistency.
- **Chapter 5: Copyright and Licensing for Online Images**
    - Legal implications of using unlicensed or copyrighted images.
    - Navigating licenses: free use, royalty-free, rights-managed, and Creative Commons.
    - Tips for tracking image licenses and choosing quality resources.
- **Chapter 6: Quality Matters – The Importance of Resolution and Composition**
    - High-quality vs. low-quality images: Understanding pixels, resolution, and appeal.

- Why your phone camera shots and stock images need editing for brand consistency.
- Editing basics to enhance any image's look and fit.

- **Chapter 7: Image Accessibility – Making Visuals Inclusive for All Users**
  - Creating alt text, readable contrast, and designs accessible to all.
  - Ensuring images meet accessibility standards to broaden engagement.
  - Tools for testing image accessibility and examples of inclusive design.
- **Chapter 8: Engagement-Driven Graphic Design – Visuals that Encourage Interaction**
  - The role of interactive elements to increase user interaction.
  - Designing clickable graphics, sharable content, and engaging visual CTAs.
  - Case studies showing how design can drive more comments, shares, and clicks.
- **Chapter 9: The Psychology of Image Placement and Composition**
  - Eye direction, visual flow, and the impact of image alignment.

    - Testing visuals across devices to maintain quality and readability.
- **Chapter 13: Measuring Graphic Performance – Analyzing What Works**
    - Using analytics to determine graphic effectiveness.
    - A/B testing and tracking engagement metrics for image performance.
    - Step-by-step examples of testing visuals to refine strategy.
- **Resource Directory: Where to Find Quality Images and Graphics**
    - Trusted sources for free and premium images.
    - Tips on licensing, copyright basics, and legal considerations.
    - Tools for editing, optimizing, and customizing images.
- **Bibliography & Recommended Reading**
    - Books, articles, and studies on graphic design, online marketing, and visual psychology.

# Introduction: The Power of Visuals in Online Marketing

When it comes to building an online presence, visuals aren't just an extra touch – they're essential. In a world where users are flooded with content every second, eye-catching and well-placed graphics can mean the difference between gaining a loyal follower and losing them in a sea of noise. Think about it: a strong, memorable image can convey a message, trigger an emotion, or create a brand impression in a split second – faster than words ever could.

## Why Visuals Matter

The internet is a visual-first environment. Platforms like Instagram, Facebook, and even LinkedIn are prioritizing visual content, making it clear that if you want to compete, your images have to be sharp, consistent, and engaging. Whether you're sharing a blog post, posting on social media, or building a landing page, the graphics you choose tell your audience more than just the literal content of the image. They communicate your brand's personality, professionalism, and even the value of what you're offering.

But let's be clear – not all visuals are created equal. Just slapping any image on a post won't cut it. Low-quality, poorly chosen visuals can turn visitors off and even hurt your credibility. On the flip side, a thoughtfully selected and well-designed graphic can capture attention, establish credibility, and drive action.

## What This Book Will Cover

In this book, we're going to dive deep into everything you need to know about choosing, creating, and using graphics that work. We'll start with the basics – understanding the different file types, how to optimize image sizes for web and mobile, and why those details matter for performance and SEO. Then, we'll move into the psychology of image placement, showing you how to guide your viewer's attention exactly where you want it.

We'll also touch on some of the finer points of online visuals, like maintaining brand consistency, navigating copyright, and making images accessible to all users. And for those who want to measure their results, we'll explore ways to track which images perform best and how to tweak your graphics based on what you learn.

## How to Use This Guide

Whether you're a small business owner, a marketer, or a social media manager, think of this book as your practical go-to guide for graphics. You don't have to be a designer to make smart choices that will make your visuals pop and support your brand – you just need the right tools and insights. Each chapter is packed with real-world tips, examples, and resources to make this as hands-on as possible.

By the end, you'll have everything you need to create stunning, effective visuals that make a real impact. So let's get started and make your graphics work harder for you!

## About the Author: Frank E. Deardurff III – That One Web Guy

Frank E. Deardurff III, also known as "That One Web Guy," is a seasoned web developer, marketer, and online business coach with over 30 years of experience in the world of graphics and digital design. With a degree in drafting, a decade of expertise in desktop publishing and technical illustration, and a lifelong passion for creating art across various mediums, Frank brings a unique perspective to visual communication.

For the past 20+ years, Frank has focused on digital graphics, mastering everything from web design and book cover creation to business cards, billboards, and everything in between. His deep understanding of how visuals work in a digital space allows him to craft designs that captivate audiences and drive results.

In addition to his extensive graphics background, Frank has more than two decades of experience helping entrepreneurs succeed online. Known for his ability to simplify complex technical topics, Frank has worked with some of the biggest names in online marketing, building, reviewing, and optimizing countless websites. His strategies focus on creating high-converting sites that not only look great but also perform exceptionally well.

Frank is also the author of “50 Biggest Website Mistakes,” “Unlocking Website Profits,” and other titles that have cemented his reputation as a trusted resource for small business owners, entrepreneurs, and marketing professionals. He’s a sought-after speaker at marketing and business events, where he shares actionable insights to help businesses grow online.

With "Visual Impact," Frank combines his decades of experience in both graphics and web design to provide readers with the tools they need to create stunning, effective visuals for websites and social media. This book is a culmination of his lifelong dedication to design and his mission to help businesses succeed through the power of impactful graphics.

# Chapter 1: File Types 101 – Choosing the Right Format for the Job

When it comes to graphics, choosing the right file type is critical. Each format serves a specific purpose, offering unique benefits and limitations. The wrong choice can result in slower load times, poor image quality, or even compatibility issues, all of which affect your audience's experience and your online performance. This chapter will break down the most common file types – JPEG, PNG, GIF, SVG, and WebP – and guide you on when to use each one.

## Why File Type Matters

File types may sound technical, but the choice you make impacts how your website or social media post performs. Different file types vary in quality, size, and purpose. A high-resolution image that looks sharp on a desktop may take ages to load on mobile if it's saved in the wrong format. Alternatively, using the wrong format could strip away the quality of a detailed graphic, giving it a blurry or pixelated look.

In online marketing, every second counts. A few extra seconds of loading time can turn visitors away, especially on mobile devices where attention spans are short. Knowing the strengths and weaknesses of each file type allows you to strike a balance between quality and performance, making sure your images look professional without slowing down your site.

## JPEG (or JPG) – The Versatile Workhorse

**Best For:** Photographs and detailed images with lots of colors
**Avoid For:** Images that need transparency or sharp, clean lines

JPEG, short for Joint Photographic Experts Group, is one of the most common image formats on the web. It's perfect for photos or images with gradients and a lot of colors. JPEG files can be compressed to reduce file size, making them quick to load, even for larger images.

**Pros:**

- **Compression:** JPEGs can be compressed heavily, reducing file size significantly.
- **Universal Compatibility:** Almost every device and browser supports JPEG files.

**Cons:**

- **Quality Loss:** JPEG compression is lossy, meaning it sacrifices some quality every time you save it.
- **No Transparency:** JPEGs don't support transparent backgrounds, so they aren't ideal for logos or icons.

**When to Use JPEG:** Choose JPEG when you need high-quality images for photography or other detailed images that don't require sharp lines or transparency. For example, a product photo for an online store works well as a JPEG – it keeps the file size manageable while maintaining detail and color.

## PNG – The Detail and Transparency Specialist

**Best For:** Images that need transparency, logos, and graphics with sharp edges
**Avoid For:** Very large images, as file sizes can get quite big

Portable Network Graphics, or PNG, is ideal when you need lossless quality and the ability to handle transparency. PNG files preserve image details and can have transparent backgrounds, which is perfect for logos, icons, and overlay images on websites.

**Pros:**

- **Transparency:** PNG supports transparent backgrounds, which is useful for overlaying graphics on various backgrounds.
- **Lossless Compression:** PNGs retain quality without losing data, which means they look crisp and clean.

**Cons:**

- **Large File Size:** Because it's lossless, PNG images can be large and may slow down load times on web pages.
- **Limited Color for PNG-8:** PNG-8 has a smaller color palette (up to 256 colors), which can make photos look flat or grainy.

**When to Use PNG:** Use PNG for graphics with text, logos, or transparent backgrounds, like icons. For instance, if you're designing a logo with a transparent background to place over different colored web sections, PNG is your go-to format.

## GIF – Animation and Simplicity

**Best For:** Simple animations, icons, and low-color images
**Avoid For:** Photos or highly detailed images

Graphics Interchange Format, or GIF, is known for its animation capabilities. It's often used for simple moving images on social media or websites, like loading icons or reaction GIFs. However, GIFs have a limited color palette, which makes them unsuitable for detailed images like photos.

**Pros:**

- **Animation:** GIFs support basic animation, which makes them ideal for short, looping visuals.
- **Small File Sizes:** With a limited color palette, GIFs are often small, which makes them load quickly.

**Cons:**

- **Limited Colors:** GIFs only support up to 256 colors, which can make them look grainy or pixelated.
- **No Smooth Transitions:** GIF animations lack smooth transitions, often resulting in a choppy appearance.

**When to Use GIF:** GIFs are ideal for short, repetitive animations, such as a loading icon or a quick demonstration of a product feature. On social media, GIFs can add personality and engagement without taking up much space or loading time.

## SVG – The Scale-Perfect Vector

**Best For:** Logos, icons, and illustrations that need to be scalable
**Avoid For:** Photographic images

Scalable Vector Graphics (SVG) are a bit different from the other file types because they're vector-based. Instead of pixels, SVGs are made of paths defined by mathematical equations, which means they can be scaled to any size without losing quality.

**Pros:**

- **Infinite Scalability:** SVGs remain crisp and clear at any size, from tiny icons to large banners.
- **Small File Size:** SVGs are typically smaller than other formats, especially for logos or icons.

- **Editability:** SVG files can be manipulated directly in code, which is helpful for web developers.

**Cons:**

- **Complexity Limitations:** SVGs aren't ideal for complex images like photos, as they don't capture fine details.
- **Browser Compatibility:** Although mostly universal, older browsers may not fully support SVGs.

**When to Use SVG:** SVG is perfect for logos, icons, and illustrations that need to be used in different sizes. For example, an SVG logo will look just as sharp on a business card as it will on a billboard.

## How to Choose the Right Format

Here's a quick decision-making process to help you decide:

1. **What's the Image Content?**
    - **Photos:** Use JPEG for a balance between quality and file size.
    - **Graphics or Logos with Text:** PNG for transparency and sharp lines, or SVG for scalability.

2. **Where Will It Be Used?**
    - **Web Pages:** For background images or product shots, opt for JPEGs or compressed PNGs to keep load times down.
    - **Social Media:** PNG for profile images and icons, GIF for simple animations, and JPEG for photos.
    - **Print:** High-resolution JPEG or SVG for vector graphics.
3. **Does It Need Transparency?**
    - PNG or SVG is your best choice if the image needs to be placed over different backgrounds.

## WebP – The Modern, Web-Optimized Format

**Best For:** Web images that need high quality with smaller file sizes
**Avoid For:** Scenarios where full browser compatibility is critical (e.g., older browsers)

WebP, developed by Google, is specifically designed for web use, combining the benefits of both JPEG and PNG. It offers both lossy and lossless compression, meaning you can maintain quality while reducing file size significantly, which is a major plus for website performance. WebP supports transparency (like PNG) and even animation (like GIF), making it a versatile option for many types of images.

**Pros:**

- **Smaller File Size:** WebP files are often 25-35% smaller than comparable JPEG or PNG files, helping your pages load faster.
- **Quality Options:** WebP offers both lossy and lossless compression, so you can choose based on your needs.
- **Supports Transparency and Animation:** Like PNG and GIF, WebP can handle transparent backgrounds and animations, making it useful for various types of graphics.

**Cons:**

- **Compatibility Issues:** While WebP is supported by most modern browsers (Chrome, Firefox, Edge), some older browsers, like certain versions of Safari and Internet Explorer, don't support it.
- **Editing and Converting Limitations:** Not all design programs support WebP natively, so you

might need to convert files to JPEG or PNG for editing.

**When to Use WebP:** WebP is ideal for any web-based images where you want high quality without the large file size. It's a great choice for blog images, product photos, and other visuals that prioritize fast load times without sacrificing detail. However, be sure to offer fallback options (like JPEG or PNG) for any users on unsupported browsers.

## A Note on Browser Compatibility

Because WebP isn't universally supported, consider using responsive image techniques to offer alternative formats for browsers that don't support it. Many Content Management Systems (CMS), like WordPress, can automate this process or have plugins available to help.

## Summary

Choosing the right file format isn't just a technical detail – it's a key part of your brand's online presence and web strategy. The format you pick affects load times, visual quality, SEO performance, and the overall user experience on your website. By understanding when to use JPEG, PNG, GIF, SVG, and modern formats like WebP, you'll make smarter choices that not only enhance your brand's appearance but also improve your site's functionality and speed. In the next chapter, we'll explore why file sizes and compression are just as crucial to maintaining a fast, well-functioning website and delivering an exceptional user experience.

# Chapter 2: The Right Size Matters – File Sizes and Load Times

When it comes to creating a seamless and enjoyable online experience, file size is just as important as file type. Even the most stunning image can turn into frustration if it takes too long to load. With today's internet users having shorter attention spans and expecting quick loading times, optimizing image file sizes is crucial. This chapter will cover why file size matters, how to compress images without sacrificing quality, and practical tips for resizing images for different platforms.

## Why File Size Matters for Performance and SEO

Every second counts on the web. Studies show that if a website takes more than three seconds to load, over half of visitors will abandon the page. Large image files are one of the biggest culprits in slowing down websites, especially when users are on mobile devices or slower networks. Beyond user experience, page speed is also a factor in SEO; search engines like Google rank faster websites higher in search results.

When you optimize file sizes, you're not just making your site faster—you're making it easier to find in search engines, and you're providing a better experience for users. Small improvements in load time can lead to lower bounce rates, higher engagement, and better conversion rates.

## Understanding Compression: Lossy vs. Lossless

**Compression** is the process of reducing the file size of an image. There are two main types of compression: **lossy** and **lossless**.

- **Lossy Compression:** In lossy compression, some data is permanently removed from the image file to reduce size. While this results in smaller files, it also causes a slight reduction in image quality. JPEG files often use lossy compression, which is why they're lightweight but may lose some fine details.
- **Lossless Compression:** Lossless compression reduces file size without sacrificing any data or quality. PNG and WebP offer lossless

compression options, preserving details and clarity while reducing size. However, lossless files are typically larger than lossy-compressed files.

Choosing between lossy and lossless compression depends on your specific needs. If the image requires high detail (like a product photo with intricate details), lossless may be better. For general images on web pages where size is a priority, lossy compression often makes sense.

## Tools for Compressing Images

You don't need to be a graphic designer to reduce file sizes effectively. Numerous tools can help you compress images with minimal quality loss. Here are a few popular options:

- **TinyPNG** and **TinyJPG**: These online tools are easy to use and support PNG and JPEG formats, offering smart lossy compression that reduces file size without sacrificing too much quality.
- **ImageOptim**: Great for Mac users, ImageOptim compresses PNG, JPEG, and GIF files. It also strips out unnecessary metadata to make files even smaller.

- **Photoshop**: Adobe Photoshop offers "Save for Web" options, allowing you to adjust quality and compression settings to get the best balance of size and quality.
- **Photopea:** Similar to Photoshop but a free web application that allows you to save smaller file sizes.
- **Squoosh** (from Google): This web-based tool supports multiple file formats and offers a slider to preview compression effects in real time.
- **WordPress Plugins**: If you're using WordPress, plugins like Smush, Imagify, and one I use frequently, WP-Optimize which can automate image compression on upload, saving you time and effort.

These tools make it easy to compress images before you upload them, ensuring that you aren't compromising load times with heavy files.

## Choosing the Right Resolution for Each Platform

Each online platform has different requirements when it comes to image resolution. Posting a high-resolution image where it isn't necessary can lead to oversized files. Here's a quick guide to optimal resolutions for common platforms:

- **Websites:** For typical web use, images are often scaled to fit within a screen's dimensions, so aim for around **72-96 DPI** (dots per inch). The goal is a balance: sharp enough to look good, but small enough to load fast. For hero images or banners, try to stay around **1200-1600 pixels wide**.
- **Social Media:** Platforms like Instagram, Facebook, and Twitter have their own recommended image sizes, usually measured in pixels. Instagram, for instance, recommends **1080 x 1080 pixels** for standard posts, while Twitter's header image should be **1500 x 500 pixels**. Using these recommended dimensions ensures your images display well without unnecessary size.
- **Email Marketing:** Email clients can be sensitive to file sizes. Aim for a maximum of **600 pixels wide** for images in newsletters or promotional emails and keep file sizes below **1 MB** to ensure smooth loading across devices.

## Strategies for Reducing File Size Without Sacrificing Quality

1. **Choose the Right Dimensions First:** Start with the size you actually need. Resizing a large image down to the right dimensions before uploading it will avoid unnecessary data.
2. **Experiment with Compression Levels:** Tools like TinyPNG and Photoshop allow you to tweak compression levels. Experiment with different levels to find the right balance between quality and size.
3. **Convert to Modern Formats When Possible:** For images intended for the web, using formats like **WebP** can significantly reduce file size without much visible quality loss. Just remember to include fallback options for unsupported browsers.
4. **Reduce Metadata:** Many image files contain extra metadata, like the camera used, location, and date taken. Tools like ImageOptim can strip out this data, saving space without affecting the image's appearance.
5. **Avoid Unnecessary Transparency:** PNG files with transparency are often larger than those without. If transparency isn't needed, try using JPEG or a non-transparent PNG to reduce file size.

## Automating Image Compression for Websites

If you're managing a large website with frequent image uploads, it may be worth investing in automated image optimization. Content Management Systems like WordPress offer plugins that compress images as they're uploaded. This way, every new image is optimized for performance without any extra work on your part.

### Popular WordPress plugins include:

- **Smush:** Automatically compresses images on upload and allows bulk optimization of existing images.
- **Imagify:** Offers different levels of compression, including lossless, and can convert images to WebP.
- **ShortPixel:** Reduces file sizes and offers options for WebP conversion and removing metadata.
- **WP-Optimize:** Is a free WordPress plugin that can help improve site speed, cache, and images.

By automating compression, you can keep your site's performance in top shape while saving time.

## Testing Load Times and Performance

It's always wise to test your site's performance to see if your images are optimized effectively. Free tools like **Google PageSpeed Insights** and **GTmetrix** provide a breakdown of how images and other files impact load times. These tools will identify which images need resizing or compression and suggest improvements.

Page speed tests can give you insight into how your images affect performance and what changes could lead to faster load times.

## Summary

Optimizing image sizes may seem like a small detail, but it's essential for a fast, user-friendly website. By understanding the basics of compression, choosing the right resolution, and using tools for efficient resizing, you're setting yourself up for a site that looks great and loads quickly. As a result, your audience will enjoy a smoother experience, and search engines will reward your site with better rankings.

In the next chapter, we'll dive into image dimensions and why choosing the right dimensions is just as important as file size.

# Chapter 3: Image Dimensions Demystified – Getting Fit for Every Platform

Have you ever visited a website where images looked stretched, cropped, or out of place? These issues are often due to using the wrong dimensions for images, which can make even high-quality graphics appear unprofessional. This chapter will help you understand why proper image dimensions are essential and how to resize images for various platforms to achieve a polished look.

## Why Image Dimensions Matter

Image dimensions refer to the width and height of an image, typically measured in pixels. The dimensions you choose impact how the image appears across devices and platforms. Choosing the wrong dimensions can lead to several issues:

- **Distorted Images:** Stretching or compressing images to fit a space can cause them to look blurry or misshapen.
- **Cropping Issues:** Social media platforms, for example, may crop images that don't match

their recommended dimensions, cutting off essential parts.

- **Slower Load Times:** Images that are too large for their display area unnecessarily consume bandwidth, slowing down page loads.

Proper dimensions ensure that images load quickly, display crisply, and appear well-positioned. Choosing the correct dimensions for each platform allows you to create a cohesive, professional look that enhances user experience.

## Practical Tips for Resizing Images

Resizing images isn't just about making them smaller or larger. It's about maintaining the aspect ratio and image quality so the visuals remain sharp and clear. Here's a practical guide for resizing without sacrificing quality:

1. **Maintain Aspect Ratio:** Aspect ratio refers to the relationship between an image's width and height. Keeping the aspect ratio consistent prevents distortion. Most image editors allow you to "lock" the aspect ratio, so changes to one dimension automatically adjust the other.
2. **Use High-Resolution Originals:** Start with a high-resolution image, as enlarging a small

image reduces quality. Begin with the highest quality version you have, then resize it down if needed.

3. **Choose the Right Dimensions First:** Decide on the final display size of your image before resizing. For example, if you need an image to fit a social media header, look up the specific dimensions recommended by the platform (e.g., 1500x500 pixels for Twitter).
4. **Export in the Correct Format:** Save images in the appropriate format after resizing. PNG or JPEG work well for most web images, while SVG is ideal for vector graphics that need to be resized frequently.

## Recommended Dimensions for Major Platforms

Each social media platform and web application has its own image requirements. Below are the recommended dimensions for popular platforms:

- **Facebook:**
    - **Profile Picture:** 180 x 180 pixels
    - **Cover Photo:** 820 x 312 pixels (desktop), 640 x 360 pixels (mobile)
    - **Shared Image:** 1200 x 630 pixels
    - **Event Cover:** 1920 x 1005 pixels

- **Instagram:**
    - **Profile Picture:** 320 x 320 pixels
    - **Standard Post:** 1080 x 1080 pixels
    - **Landscape Post:** 1080 x 566 pixels
    - **Portrait Post:** 1080 x 1350 pixels
    - **Story:** 1080 x 1920 pixels
- **Twitter:**
    - **Profile Picture:** 400 x 400 pixels
    - **Header Image:** 1500 x 500 pixels
    - **In-Stream Image:** 1600 x 900 pixels
- **LinkedIn:**
    - **Profile Picture:** 400 x 400 pixels
    - **Background Photo:** 1584 x 396 pixels
    - **Shared Image (Post):** 1200 x 627 pixels
    - **Company Logo:** 300 x 300 pixels
- **Pinterest:**
    - **Profile Picture:** 165 x 165 pixels
    - **Pin:** 1000 x 1500 pixels (recommended aspect ratio is 2:3)
    - **Board Cover:** 600 x 600 pixels
- **YouTube:**
    - **Profile Picture:** 800 x 800 pixels
    - **Channel Cover:** 2560 x 1440 pixels (optimized for desktop)
    - **Video Thumbnail:** 1280 x 720 pixels
- **Web Banners and Images:**

    - **Hero Image (homepage banner):** 1200 x 600 pixels (varies by website design)
    - **Product Image:** 800 x 800 pixels (or larger for zoom capability)

Using these recommended dimensions ensures your images display properly, keeping your visuals sharp and on-brand.

## Adapting Images for Mobile Devices

With over half of all web traffic coming from mobile devices, optimizing images for mobile is essential. Mobile screens are typically smaller and have different aspect ratios than desktops, which can impact how images display. Here are some tips for mobile optimization:

- **Use Responsive Design:** Responsive design automatically adjusts image size based on the user's screen. Tools like CSS media queries or WordPress plugins can help you achieve a responsive layout.
- **Focus on Readability:** On small screens, text within images should be large and readable. Avoid cramming too much text or small details that could be hard to see on a phone.

- **Test Across Devices:** Use tools like Google's Mobile-Friendly Test or BrowserStack to see how your images appear on different devices.

By adapting your images for mobile, you ensure a seamless user experience, no matter how visitors access your content.

## Tools for Resizing Images

Several tools make resizing images easy, even if you don't have design experience. Here are a few recommendations:

- **Canva:** Canva offers templates for social media posts, headers, and more, with preset dimensions for different platforms.
- **Photoshop:** Adobe Photoshop allows precise control over image size and resolution, making it ideal for complex resizing needs.
- **Photopea:** A free alternative to Photoshop.
- **Pixlr:** A free, browser-based editor that lets you resize images with simple controls.
- **Figma:** A great option for collaborative design, Figma allows you to set exact dimensions and scale images without losing quality.
- **GIMP:** An open-source image editor with resizing options for various platforms.

Using these tools, you can easily resize images to match the ideal dimensions for any platform.

## Testing Image Dimensions and Placement

When preparing images for websites and social media, testing how they'll look in their intended location is essential. Upload images in preview mode to see if they fit well and display as expected. Many platforms allow you to preview your post or web page before publishing, giving you a chance to catch any issues with cropping, sizing, or positioning.

## Summary

Understanding and choosing the right image dimensions is more than a matter of aesthetics. It's a key part of your brand's online presence and affects everything from page speed to user experience. By following the recommended dimensions for each platform, using responsive design for mobile users, and testing images before publishing, you'll ensure that every graphic looks professional, sharp, and well-suited to its platform.

In the next chapter, we'll focus on brand consistency and explore why maintaining a cohesive look across all graphics can strengthen your brand identity.

# Chapter 4: Brand Consistency in Visuals

In the crowded online landscape, building a recognizable and trustworthy brand is crucial. Visual consistency is one of the easiest ways to make your brand instantly identifiable, even before someone reads your content. Think about it: when you see the iconic red and white of Coca-Cola or the sleek minimalism of Apple, you recognize them right away. That's the power of brand consistency.

This chapter will dive into why maintaining a cohesive look across all visuals matters and how to create a visual style guide to keep your brand consistent.

## Why Brand Consistency Matters

Consistency in branding isn't just about looking good – it's about building trust and reliability. When your audience sees consistent visuals, they subconsciously associate them with your brand, making it easier to remember and recognize. This consistency creates a sense of familiarity, which is key to building trust over time.

Some of the main benefits of brand consistency in visuals include:

- **Improved Brand Recognition:** Consistent visuals make your brand instantly recognizable, whether someone sees it on your website, social media, or in an email.
- **Enhanced Professionalism:** A unified look conveys a sense of professionalism and attention to detail, setting you apart from competitors.
- **Increased Engagement:** Audiences are more likely to engage with visuals that feel cohesive and aligned with the brand's message.

In short, a consistent brand experience fosters a sense of reliability and helps you build a loyal following.

## Key Elements of a Visual Style Guide

A visual style guide is a reference document that lays out the design principles for your brand's visuals. It's especially useful if you work with multiple designers or contributors, as it ensures everyone is on the same page about your brand's look and feel. Here are the core elements to include in your style guide:

1. **Logo Usage**
    - **Primary and Secondary Logos:** Define where to use the main logo versus alternate versions (like monochrome or icon-only).
    - **Spacing and Placement:** Include guidelines on logo spacing to prevent crowding and specify where to place logos within images (e.g., always in the top-left corner).
    - **Size and Scaling:** Provide minimum and maximum sizes to keep your logo readable and prevent distortion.
2. **Color Palette**
    - **Primary Colors:** Choose two to three core colors that represent your brand, and include their hex codes, RGB, and CMYK values for consistency across digital and print.
    - **Secondary Colors:** Pick complementary colors that can be used for accents or backgrounds, but limit their use to avoid visual clutter.
    - **Neutral Colors:** Define neutral tones like white, black, or gray for text, backgrounds, and contrast.

3. **Typography**
   - **Fonts:** Choose one or two fonts for headers and body text, along with any specific uses (e.g., bold for headings, italic for quotes).
   - **Font Sizes and Spacing:** Set guidelines for font sizes, line spacing, and alignment to keep text uniform across graphics.
   - **Alternative Fonts:** Include acceptable alternatives for cases when your main fonts aren't available, such as on certain web platforms.
4. **Image Style and Filters**
   - **Types of Images:** Decide if you'll primarily use photos, illustrations, or icons and establish a consistent style. For example, candid photos with natural light or vector icons with flat design.
   - **Filters and Effects:** Specify any filters, overlays, or effects that should be applied to maintain a uniform look, such as a specific saturation level or light vignette.
   - **Photo Composition:** If using photos, decide on angles, focus, or framing guidelines (e.g., close-ups with blurred

backgrounds or photos with subjects centered).

5. **Iconography and Graphics**
    - **Icon Style:** If your brand uses icons, establish whether they should be flat, line-based, filled, etc., and ensure they align with the overall aesthetic.
    - **Graphic Elements:** Define any repeating graphic elements, such as lines, borders, or shapes, and where they should be placed within designs.
    - **Size and Placement:** Include size and placement rules for icons or graphics to maintain a balanced look within images or alongside text.
6. **Voice and Tone**
    - **Mood of Visuals:** Visuals should reflect the brand's tone of voice. For example, a wellness brand might use soft, calming images, while a tech brand may prefer sleek, futuristic visuals.
    - **Emotional Appeal:** Decide if visuals should be aspirational, relatable, humorous, or serious, and aim to evoke a consistent emotion.

By creating a style guide with these elements, you ensure your visuals are recognizable and reinforce your brand's identity.

## Practical Steps to Build and Maintain Consistency

Consistency doesn't happen overnight. It requires a systematic approach to ensure your visuals align with your brand message across all platforms. Here's how to start:

1. **Audit Your Current Visuals:** Before setting a new standard, review your current images and graphics. Identify inconsistencies in colors, fonts, and styles, and note what feels "on-brand" versus what doesn't.
2. **Define Your Visual Identity:** Use the elements in your style guide to solidify your brand's look. This will act as the visual "face" of your brand, making it easier for your audience to connect with and remember you.
3. **Create Templates for Repetitive Content:** Templates for social media posts, email headers, and blog images can help you maintain a consistent look with minimal effort.

Many platforms, like Canva or Adobe Express, allow you to save templates for repeated use.
4. **Educate Your Team:** Share the style guide with everyone involved in creating content for your brand. When everyone understands the guidelines, it's easier to ensure a unified look.
5. **Use Automation Tools for Branding Consistency:** If you're managing visuals across multiple platforms, automation tools like Buffer or Hootsuite can help maintain a uniform brand appearance by scheduling and managing content in a single space.

## Real-World Examples of Brand Consistency

Sometimes, seeing consistency in action helps drive home the importance of these guidelines. Here are a few brands known for their cohesive and instantly recognizable visuals:

- **Coca-Cola:** With its distinct red, white, and classic script font, Coca-Cola's branding is consistent across every platform. Their visuals often evoke a sense of nostalgia and community, which aligns with their brand message.

- **Apple:** Apple maintains a minimalist aesthetic with neutral tones, sleek product images, and a refined color palette. Their use of white space, sharp product images, and clean lines reinforces their brand as modern and cutting-edge.
- **Nike:** Known for bold, energetic visuals, Nike consistently uses powerful images of athletes that reflect their message of motivation and perseverance. Their signature "swoosh" logo is placed strategically across visuals, creating an instant brand association.

By analyzing these brands, you can see how consistency builds a strong, recognizable presence.

## Keeping Your Visuals Fresh Without Breaking Consistency

Over time, brands evolve, and visual styles may need to be updated to stay relevant. Here are some ways to refresh your visuals while maintaining consistency:

- **Evolve Gradually:** Instead of a complete overhaul, make gradual updates to your colors, fonts, or images to avoid alienating your existing audience.

- **Introduce Seasonal Variations:** Create alternate templates or color schemes for special events, holidays, or seasons, while still adhering to your main guidelines.
- **A/B Test New Ideas:** If you're considering a change, run A/B tests on visuals to see if your audience responds positively. This feedback helps you make informed choices without disrupting brand identity.

## Summary

Brand consistency in visuals isn't just about looking polished – it's a strategic tool for building recognition, trust, and engagement. By creating a style guide and following a few practical steps, you can ensure that your brand's personality and professionalism shine through every visual, on every platform.

In the next chapter, we'll explore copyright and licensing, so you can be confident that your brand's visuals are both consistent and legally compliant.

# Chapter 5: Copyright and Licensing for Online Images

In today's digital age, finding high-quality images is easier than ever – but using them legally is a whole different story. Copyright and licensing can seem like complex topics, but understanding them is essential to protect your brand from legal risks and ensure you're using images responsibly. This chapter will explain the basics of copyright, the different types of licenses, and best practices for legally using images online.

## What is Copyright?

Copyright is a legal protection given to creators of original works, including photos, illustrations, and other images. When someone takes a photo or creates an illustration, they automatically hold the copyright to that image, giving them exclusive rights to use, share, and sell it. Copyright protection applies to all original images, whether they're found on the internet, social media, or a stock photo site.

If you use an image without permission from the copyright holder, you're at risk of copyright infringement, which can result in fines or legal action. That's why it's crucial to understand licensing before using images in your online content.

## Types of Image Licenses

Not all licenses are created equal. Different licenses grant different rights, and understanding each type helps you make informed decisions about image use. Here's a breakdown of common licenses and what they mean:

1. **Royalty-Free License**
   - **Definition:** With a royalty-free (RF) license, you pay a one-time fee to use an image multiple times, without additional costs.
   - **Limitations:** You can't claim ownership of the image, and there may be restrictions on using it for resale products (like t-shirts or mugs).
   - **Best For:** Websites, blogs, and social media content where you need flexibility.
2. **Rights-Managed License**
   - **Definition:** Rights-managed (RM) licenses give you the right to use an image in a specific way, such as for a

particular project or for a limited period. Each use requires a separate license.
  - **Limitations:** This license type is restrictive and often comes with higher fees, especially for commercial uses.
  - **Best For:** Projects where you need exclusive rights or control over how the image is used.

3. **Creative Commons (CC) License**
  - **Definition:** Creative Commons licenses allow creators to specify how others can use their work, typically with fewer restrictions than traditional copyright.
  - **Types of CC Licenses:** Creative Commons licenses come in different types, including:
    - **CC BY (Attribution):** Free to use with credit to the creator.
    - **CC BY-SA (ShareAlike):** Free to use, share, and modify with credit; modifications must be shared under the same license.
    - **CC BY-NC (NonCommercial):** Free to use for non-commercial purposes with credit.
    - **CC0 (Public Domain):** Free to use without credit or restrictions.

    - **Best For:** Content creators looking for free, flexible image options.
4. **Public Domain**
    - **Definition:** Images in the public domain are free to use without restrictions because their copyright has expired or the creator has waived rights.
    - **Limitations:** None; public domain images can be used, modified, and distributed freely.
    - **Best For:** Any project where you need unrestricted image use.
5. **Custom License Agreements**
    - **Definition:** Some photographers or agencies offer custom licenses, which specify exactly how you're allowed to use an image. These agreements are often negotiated and tailored to specific needs.
    - **Best For:** Unique projects or long-term usage where you need specific rights or exclusivity.

Understanding these licenses helps you choose images that fit your project requirements without risking copyright infringement.

## Finding and Using Licensed Images

Now that you know the basics of licensing, let's look at where to find images that are safe to use. Here are a few popular sources and tips for making sure your images are properly licensed:

1. **Stock Photo Sites**
    - **Examples:** Shutterstock, Adobe Stock, iStock
    - **License Types:** Stock sites typically offer royalty-free licenses, but some also have rights-managed options.
    - **Best Practices:** Check the license terms for each image, as some stock sites have limitations on commercial use or redistribution.
2. **Creative Commons Sites**
    - **Examples:** Unsplash, Pexels, Pixabay
    - **License Types:** These sites often use Creative Commons or custom licenses, allowing free use with certain conditions.
    - **Best Practices:** Always read the specific license details. Some images require attribution, while others are free to use without credit.

3. **Public Domain Archives**
    - **Examples:** Wikimedia Commons, PublicDomainPictures.net, Library of Congress
    - **License Types:** Images in public domain archives are free of copyright restrictions.
    - **Best Practices:** Although public domain images are free to use, it's a good idea to double-check that no copyright restrictions apply.
4. **Original Photography and Graphic Design**
    - **Definition:** Creating your own images ensures you have complete control and ownership over the content.
    - **Best Practices:** If you or your team can take original photos or create graphics, it's often the safest route, as it eliminates any licensing concerns.
5. **Social Media Images**
    - **Caution:** Just because an image is on social media doesn't mean it's free to use. Using someone else's image without permission can result in copyright infringement.

- **Best Practices:** Seek permission from the creator, or use images from social media that are shared under a Creative Commons license.

## How to Properly Attribute Images

When using images that require attribution (such as many Creative Commons images), proper crediting is essential. Failing to give credit can violate the license terms and may lead to copyright issues. Here's a simple format for attributing images:

1. **Credit the Creator:** Include the name of the photographer or artist.
2. **Link to the Source:** If possible, link to the original source of the image.
3. **License Information:** State the type of license (e.g., "Image licensed under CC BY 4.0").

Example attribution: *Photo by Jane Doe on Unsplash (CC BY 4.0)*

Many stock photo sites provide attribution guidelines for each image, so check their recommendations to ensure compliance.

## Protecting Your Brand from Copyright Infringement

Copyright infringement can be costly and damaging to your brand's reputation. Here are some best practices to protect your brand:

1. **Read License Agreements Carefully:** Never assume an image is free to use. Always check the license and understand its terms.
2. **Track Image Licenses:** Keep a record of the licenses for each image you use, including screenshots or downloaded licenses for future reference.
3. **Avoid Derivative Works Without Permission:** Modifying an image doesn't automatically make it copyright-free. Some licenses prohibit derivative works, so check the terms before editing or transforming an image.
4. **Use Reverse Image Search:** If you're unsure of an image's origin, use tools like Google Reverse Image Search or TinEye to locate the source and check for licensing.
5. **Invest in Professional Licensing Services:** If your brand uses a high volume of images, consider licensing images from reputable stock

agencies or hiring a photographer to create custom visuals.

## Handling Copyright Claims and Take-Down Notices

Despite taking precautions, you might still receive a copyright claim or take-down notice. Here's how to handle it:

1. **Review the Claim:** Carefully read the claim or notice to understand which image is in question and the specific copyright issue.
2. **Remove the Image Temporarily:** If the claim is valid or you're unsure of the license, remove the image from your site or social media to avoid further issues.
3. **Reach Out to the Claimant:** If you believe the claim is mistaken or if you have proof of licensing, contact the claimant to clarify the situation.
4. **Seek Legal Help if Necessary:** For complex claims, especially those involving potential financial penalties, consult a legal professional specializing in copyright.

By handling copyright claims responsibly, you can protect your brand's reputation and avoid legal consequences.

## Summary

Copyright and licensing may seem complicated, but understanding these principles is essential for anyone using images online. By choosing licensed images, attributing properly, and respecting copyright laws, you can confidently create visuals that elevate your brand without risking infringement. In the next chapter, we'll explore accessibility and how making visuals inclusive can broaden your audience and improve user experience.

# Chapter 6: Image Accessibility – Making Visuals Inclusive for All Users

In today's digital world, accessibility is more than a nice-to-have feature; it's essential. Making images accessible ensures that all users, including those with disabilities, can engage with your content. This chapter will cover the importance of image accessibility, best practices to make your visuals inclusive, and tools for testing accessibility. By following these guidelines, you'll improve user experience and broaden your audience reach.

## Why Image Accessibility Matters

Accessible images aren't just about compliance; they're about inclusion. Visual content is a powerful tool for communication, but it can exclude people with visual impairments if not properly formatted. By making your images accessible, you ensure that everyone can understand and enjoy your content.

Additionally, accessible images can benefit your SEO. Search engines can't "see" images the way humans do, but they can read image descriptions (alt text), which helps them understand the content and relevance of your visuals. Making your images accessible can improve your site's search ranking, potentially increasing visibility.

## Understanding Alt Text and Its Importance

**Alt text** (alternative text) is one of the most crucial elements of accessible images. Alt text is a short description that conveys the content and function of an image for users who cannot see it. Screen readers read alt text aloud to visually impaired users, enabling them to understand the image's purpose.

When writing alt text, keep the following guidelines in mind:

- **Be Descriptive:** Describe the essential details that convey the image's purpose. For example, instead of "dog," write "a golden retriever running on a beach."
- **Keep It Concise:** Aim for a brief but complete description. Typically, 125 characters or fewer is ideal for readability by screen readers.
- **Avoid Redundancy:** Do not start with "image of" or "picture of," as screen readers already announce that an image is present.

- **Consider Context:** Tailor your alt text based on the image's role within the content. If the image conveys information critical to understanding the content, include those details.

Example: For an image of a person painting a mural at a community event, alt text could be: "Artist painting a colorful mural at a community event with people watching."

## Best Practices for Accessible Images

Beyond alt text, there are several other ways to ensure your images are accessible and user-friendly:

1. **Use Descriptive Captions When Necessary**
   - Captions are visible descriptions that add context to an image. While they aren't a substitute for alt text, they provide helpful information for all users.
   - **Tip:** Use captions for complex images, such as graphs or charts, to give additional context.
2. **Include Image Descriptions for Complex Visuals**

- For images that contain intricate information, such as infographics or detailed illustrations, consider adding a longer description in the body text or as a link to a full description.
- **Example:** For an infographic on social media usage trends, include a detailed summary explaining the data in text form.

3. **Optimize Image Contrast and Readability**
   - Ensure text within images has high contrast against the background to improve readability, especially for users with visual impairments.
   - **Tip:** Use a contrast ratio of at least 4.5:1 between text and background colors, as recommended by Web Content Accessibility Guidelines (WCAG).
4. **Avoid Using Text-Heavy Images**
   - Text within images isn't accessible to screen readers, so avoid putting important information in images alone. If necessary, repeat the information in the surrounding text.
   - **Example:** If you have a promotional graphic with a call-to-action, include

the same message in a visible text element on the page.

5. **Provide Transcripts for Image-Based Content**
   - For images with a lot of embedded text, such as infographics or educational slides, consider offering a transcript or written summary so that all users can access the information.
   - **Tip:** Place the transcript or description below the image or link to it for easy access.

## Ensuring Accessibility Across Different Image Types

Not all images serve the same purpose, and each type requires unique accessibility considerations:

- **Decorative Images**: Decorative images are visuals that don't add information or context. They can be marked with empty alt text (alt="") to let screen readers skip them. This avoids distracting users with unnecessary details.
- **Functional Images**: Images that act as links or buttons need alt text that describes their

function, such as “Search icon” for a magnifying glass button.

- **Informative Images**: Informative images, such as diagrams, charts, or images conveying specific data, require descriptive alt text. Including any relevant details ensures that visually impaired users understand the information.

By addressing each type appropriately, you can ensure that every image aligns with its purpose and remains accessible.

## Tools for Testing Image Accessibility

Ensuring accessibility isn’t a one-time task – it requires regular testing and validation. Fortunately, there are tools available to help you test image accessibility:

1. **WAVE (Web Accessibility Evaluation Tool)**: WAVE is a free tool that identifies accessibility issues on web pages, including missing alt text and contrast issues.
2. **Axe Accessibility Checker**: This browser extension provides automated testing for accessibility, including checks for alt text and other image-related elements.

3. **Screen Readers**: Testing with screen readers, such as JAWS (Job Access With Speech) or NVDA (NonVisual Desktop Access), helps you experience your website as a visually impaired user would and identify areas for improvement.
4. **Color Contrast Checkers**: Tools like the WCAG Contrast Checker or Contrast Ratio help you verify that text within images meets the recommended contrast standards for readability.

Using these tools allows you to spot and fix any issues before they impact your users, ensuring a more accessible experience.

## Legal Considerations and Compliance Standards

In many regions, digital accessibility isn't just a best practice – it's a legal requirement. Various standards and regulations exist to protect the rights of individuals with disabilities:

- **WCAG (Web Content Accessibility Guidelines)**: The WCAG standards, developed by the World Wide Web Consortium (W3C), provide detailed accessibility recommendations, including alt text, contrast, and layout guidelines.

- **ADA (Americans with Disabilities Act)**: In the United States, ADA compliance includes ensuring that web content is accessible to individuals with disabilities. Non-compliance can result in legal action.
- **Section 508**: Section 508 of the Rehabilitation Act mandates that all federal websites and digital services in the U.S. be accessible to people with disabilities.

Understanding these standards helps you ensure your website is accessible, compliant, and inclusive.

## Common Pitfalls and How to Avoid Them

Even with the best intentions, accessibility mistakes happen. Here are a few common pitfalls and tips to avoid them:

1. **Using Generic Alt Text**: Alt text like "image" or "photo" isn't descriptive enough to be useful. Make sure alt text adds value and describes the content.
2. **Ignoring Decorative Images**: Failing to mark decorative images as such can clutter the

experience for screen reader users. Use empty alt text (alt="") for purely decorative visuals.

3. **Overloading Images with Text**: Text-heavy images can't be read by screen readers, so avoid using them to convey critical information. Use actual text on the webpage instead.
4. **Neglecting Mobile Accessibility**: Accessibility standards should apply to both desktop and mobile. Ensure that images are readable and accessible across devices.

By recognizing these pitfalls and making intentional adjustments, you'll improve accessibility for all users.

## Summary

Making images accessible is a crucial step toward creating an inclusive and user-friendly website. By following best practices like using alt text, ensuring contrast, and using accessibility tools, you make your content accessible to everyone, including visually impaired users. Plus, these efforts benefit your brand by enhancing SEO and ensuring compliance with accessibility standards. In the next chapter, we'll explore engagement-driven graphic design and how to create visuals that encourage users to interact with your content.

# Chapter 7: Engagement-Driven Graphic Design – Visuals That Encourage Interaction

In a world overflowing with content, capturing your audience's attention is just the first step. To build a lasting connection, your visuals must encourage engagement – inspiring people to like, comment, share, and click. Engagement-driven design goes beyond aesthetics; it focuses on creating visuals that invite action and enhance user experience.

This chapter will guide you through creating visuals that encourage interaction, why engagement matters, and strategies to drive active participation from your audience.

## Why Engagement-Driven Design Matters

Engagement-driven design isn't just about creating beautiful graphics. It's about designing visuals that resonate with users, prompting them to interact, share, or take action. Higher engagement doesn't just increase visibility; it can also boost brand loyalty, extend reach, and improve conversion rates.

Some benefits of engagement-driven design include:

- **Increased Visibility**: Engaging visuals encourage likes, shares, and comments, amplifying your reach across social platforms.
- **Stronger Connections**: Interactive designs create a personal connection with users, building a community around your brand.
- **Improved SEO**: Engagement metrics like click-through rates and shares can positively impact search rankings, especially on platforms like YouTube and Google.

Designing with engagement in mind helps you make a lasting impression that goes beyond surface-level interest.

## Principles of Engagement-Driven Design

Certain design principles naturally encourage user engagement. Incorporating these elements can create a visually appealing experience that draws viewers in and prompts action:

1. **Visual Hierarchy**
    - Organize your design with clear visual hierarchy, guiding users to the most important elements first. Techniques like contrasting colors, bold typography, or focal points can draw attention to calls-to-action (CTAs).
    - **Example**: Use a large, bold CTA button in a contrasting color to make it stand out against the background.
2. **Emotionally Resonant Imagery**
    - Images that evoke emotions, such as joy, empathy, or excitement, often lead to higher engagement. Emotionally resonant visuals create a sense of connection, prompting users to share or react.
    - **Example**: For a health brand, showing real people engaged in a healthy lifestyle can resonate emotionally, encouraging shares and comments.
3. **Authenticity and Relatability**
    - Authentic, relatable visuals make your brand feel approachable. Users are more likely to engage with content that feels

"real" rather than overly polished or staged.
    - **Example**: User-generated content, like photos from your customers, adds authenticity and often sees higher engagement than stock images.
4. **Interactive Elements**
    - Interactive elements like polls, sliders, or carousel posts invite users to participate rather than passively view. On platforms like Instagram, interactive stories can drive engagement by encouraging users to swipe or click.
    - **Example**: Use an Instagram story poll to get feedback or ask questions related to your product, fostering a sense of involvement.
5. **Clear and Compelling CTAs**
    - Every engagement-driven graphic should include a call-to-action (CTA) that directs users on what to do next. Whether it's "Swipe up," "Learn more," or "Share your thoughts," clear CTAs improve engagement rates.
    - **Example**: For a blog post preview, add a CTA like "Read the full article" with a

button that encourages clicks and directs traffic to your site.

## Types of Engagement-Driven Visuals

Not every image or graphic needs to be interactive, but certain types are naturally better at prompting engagement. Here are a few types of visuals that typically drive high interaction:

1. **Infographics**
    - Infographics break down complex information into digestible, visually appealing formats. They're highly shareable and often lead to comments, as users discuss or ask questions about the data.
    - **Design Tip**: Use a clean layout with icons and small text blocks to keep information easy to read and engaging.
2. **Behind-the-Scenes Photos**
    - Giving users a behind-the-scenes look at your brand fosters a sense of authenticity and connection. These images can prompt comments, questions, and shares, as users feel more "involved" with your brand.

- **Design Tip**: Avoid overly edited or polished photos; aim for candid shots that show real people or processes.

3. **User-Generated Content (UGC)**
   - User-generated content, such as customer photos or reviews, builds trust and invites other users to share their experiences. UGC encourages others to interact, like, or comment, as they relate to real customer stories.
   - **Design Tip**: Create a branded hashtag to encourage users to share photos of your product, which you can then feature in your posts.
4. **Polls and Quizzes**
   - Polls and quizzes invite users to participate actively, creating an interactive experience. This type of content is highly engaging, as it encourages users to reflect, share opinions, and connect with others.
   - **Design Tip**: Use simple, bold graphics with minimal text to keep polls or quiz options easy to read and quick to interact with.

5. **Contests and Giveaways**
    - Contests and giveaways prompt engagement by offering an incentive for actions like sharing, commenting, or tagging friends. They can drive a significant boost in interactions and extend your reach.
    - **Design Tip**: Create a visually appealing contest image with clear instructions and a prominent CTA, such as "Enter to Win."

## Optimizing Engagement for Different Platforms

Each platform has its own unique features, user behaviors, and engagement drivers. Here are some platform-specific tips to help you maximize engagement across major social media channels:

1. **Instagram**
    - **Stories**: Use interactive features like polls, quizzes, and questions in your Instagram Stories. These features encourage users to engage with your content in a quick, low-effort way.

    - **Carousel Posts**: Carousel posts allow you to share multiple images in one post, keeping users swiping through. Use carousels for step-by-step guides, product features, or before-and-after images.
    - **Design Tip**: Keep visuals clean and bright to match Instagram's aesthetic. Use overlays or text sparingly but make CTAs prominent.
2. **Facebook**
    - **Live Videos**: Facebook Live is a powerful way to engage users in real time. During a live video, encourage viewers to comment, react, or ask questions, which keeps them involved throughout.
    - **Posts with Questions**: Add open-ended questions to image posts or graphics to encourage comments. Questions that prompt users to share opinions or stories often lead to high engagement.
    - **Design Tip**: Facebook users respond well to both polished graphics and more candid, relatable images. Choose visuals based on your audience's preferences.

3. **Twitter**
    - **Polls**: Twitter's native poll feature is a quick way to increase engagement. Polls are easy to respond to and often prompt users to share additional thoughts in replies.
    - **GIFs and Memes**: GIFs and memes are highly shareable on Twitter, adding a sense of humor and personality to your brand. Use them to respond to current trends or engage in conversations with your audience.
    - **Design Tip**: Keep text brief and visuals eye-catching, as Twitter users often scroll quickly. Bold images with minimal text perform well.
4. **LinkedIn**
    - **Infographics and Industry Insights**: LinkedIn users appreciate valuable content related to their professional lives. Infographics that provide insights, statistics, or industry trends are often shared and discussed.
    - **Company Culture Images**: Photos that showcase your team, office culture, or events foster connection and can

prompt comments from peers and followers.
    - **Design Tip**: Use professional visuals that reflect your industry. Subtle colors, clean lines, and professional fonts align with LinkedIn's business-oriented environment.
5. **Pinterest**
    - **Vertical Images**: Pinterest favors vertical images with a 2:3 aspect ratio. High-quality vertical images capture attention and are more likely to be saved or repinned.
    - **Infographics and Step-by-Step Guides**: Detailed infographics and visual guides perform well on Pinterest. They provide value and can generate significant engagement over time.
    - **Design Tip**: Use clear, concise text overlays and vibrant colors to stand out in users' feeds. Make sure any text within images is large enough to read on mobile screens.

## Measuring the Success of Engagement-Driven Visuals

Creating engagement-driven visuals is only the first step. Measuring how well they perform helps you refine your approach and identify what resonates most with your audience. Key metrics to track include:

- **Likes and Shares**: These indicate how well your content is received and shared with a broader audience.
- **Comments**: Comments show that users are actively engaging with your content and provide insights into their thoughts or reactions.
- **Click-Through Rate (CTR)**: CTR is essential for visuals designed to drive traffic. It measures the percentage of users who clicked on a link or CTA after viewing the image.
- **Save and Bookmark Rates**: Platforms like Instagram and Pinterest allow users to save content. High save rates suggest that your content provides lasting value or inspiration.
- **Conversion Rate**: For visuals with a clear call-to-action (like "Buy Now" or "Sign Up"),

conversion rate shows the percentage of users who took the desired action.

By analyzing these metrics, you can identify which types of visuals drive the most engagement and optimize future designs accordingly.

## Summary

Engagement-driven design transforms your visuals from passive content into interactive experiences. By using principles like visual hierarchy, emotional resonance, and clear CTAs, you can create graphics that invite users to like, comment, share, and engage. Coupled with platform-specific strategies, these techniques help you connect more deeply with your audience, amplifying your brand's reach and impact.

In the next chapter, we'll explore current trends in social media graphics, so you can stay updated on what's working in today's ever-evolving visual landscape.

# Chapter 8: Leveraging Trends in Social Media Graphics

Social media is constantly evolving, with visual trends shifting as quickly as users' attention spans. Staying updated with these trends helps your brand remain relevant and can boost engagement. However, not every trend is worth adopting. In this chapter, we'll explore some of the most impactful current trends in social media graphics, how to determine if a trend aligns with your brand, and ways to incorporate trends without compromising your visual identity.

## Why Staying Current with Visual Trends Matters

Visual trends on social media capture what audiences find fresh and engaging. When you leverage these trends, you show that your brand is in tune with what's current and resonate with users who expect timely, visually appealing content. Incorporating trends strategically can:

- **Boost Engagement**: Trendy visuals often capture more attention and prompt shares, comments, and likes.

- **Enhance Relevance**: Staying current helps your brand feel contemporary and relevant in a fast-paced social media landscape.
- **Increase Reach**: Trend-driven content is often favored by platform algorithms, especially when it involves features like short-form video or interactive elements.

However, trends should support your brand's message, not overshadow it. The key is to choose trends that complement your identity rather than following every passing fad.

## Key Trends in Social Media Graphics

Here are some of the top visual trends currently dominating social media and strategies for using them effectively:

1. **Minimalist Aesthetics**
    - **What It Is**: Minimalism strips visuals down to essential elements, using clean lines, ample white space, and a limited color palette.
    - **Why It Works**: In a busy feed, minimalist designs stand out by creating a sense of calm and clarity,

drawing attention to the message or product.
    - **How to Use It**: Highlight a single product or message with ample white space and minimal text. For example, a product reveal graphic with only the product and a single CTA can create a strong impact.
2. **Bold Typography and Text-Only Graphics**
    - **What It Is**: This trend focuses on eye-catching fonts and creative text layouts, often without any supporting images.
    - **Why It Works**: Large, bold text immediately communicates key messages, making these graphics effective for announcements, quotes, or calls to action.
    - **How to Use It**: Use bold typography for messages you want to stand out, like flash sales or important updates. Experiment with playful or expressive fonts that align with your brand's tone.
3. **Muted and Pastel Color Palettes**
    - **What It Is**: Soft, muted colors and pastel tones create a calm and inviting

look, adding a modern and cohesive aesthetic to your brand.
   - **Why It Works**: These palettes convey warmth and friendliness, appealing to audiences looking for relatable, approachable brands.
   - **How to Use It**: Use pastel tones in backgrounds or as accents in your graphics. If your brand typically uses vibrant colors, try incorporating pastels as secondary colors for a fresh twist.
4. **Authentic, Candid Photography**
   - **What It Is**: Instead of polished, staged photos, this trend focuses on genuine, in-the-moment images that feel relatable and personal.
   - **Why It Works**: Audiences are increasingly drawn to authenticity, and candid photography feels more trustworthy and down-to-earth.
   - **How to Use It**: Incorporate behind-the-scenes photos of your team, workspace, or real customers using your product. Avoid heavy editing to keep the look natural and relatable.
5. **Illustrations and Custom Graphics**

    - **What It Is**: Hand-drawn illustrations and custom graphics add a unique, creative flair that sets your visuals apart.
    - **Why It Works**: Custom illustrations feel personal and original, allowing brands to tell a story or express a message in a way that's hard to replicate.
    - **How to Use It**: Consider using custom illustrations for explainer graphics, seasonal themes, or to highlight a unique aspect of your brand. They can also be great for "how-to" or "step-by-step" visuals.
6. **Short-Form Videos and Motion Graphics**
    - **What It Is**: Platforms like Instagram Reels, TikTok, and YouTube Shorts have popularized short-form videos, while motion graphics involve animated text or images within a short clip.
    - **Why It Works**: Videos are engaging and perform well on most platforms. Motion graphics allow you to add life to otherwise static visuals, increasing time spent on your content.

    - **How to Use It**: Use short-form videos for quick tutorials, product demos, or fun, engaging content. Motion graphics can be added to social posts to highlight announcements or CTAs.
7. **Carousel and Interactive Posts**
    - **What It Is**: Carousel posts allow users to swipe through multiple images in a single post, and interactive elements prompt users to engage with the content.
    - **Why It Works**: Carousels keep users engaged longer as they swipe, while interactive elements foster participation and connection.
    - **How to Use It**: Use carousels to share step-by-step guides, showcase product collections, or tell a story. Include CTAs to swipe, tap, or engage within the visuals to encourage interaction.
8. **3D and Immersive Visuals**
    - **What It Is**: 3D graphics and immersive visuals create a sense of depth and realism, adding an eye-catching, almost tactile element to digital graphics.
    - **Why It Works**: 3D graphics stand out in a feed of flat images, making them

particularly effective for product showcases or creative branding.
    - **How to Use It**: Use 3D graphics for hero images, product showcases, or branding that needs to make a memorable impact. Ensure they align with your brand's personality to avoid a disconnect.

## Determining If a Trend Fits Your Brand

Not every trend will suit your brand. Before jumping on a new style, ask yourself these questions to determine if it aligns with your brand identity:

- **Does this trend resonate with my target audience?** Think about whether your audience would find the trend appealing or if it might come across as off-brand.
- **Will this trend reinforce my brand message?** Ensure that the trend complements your core message and values rather than diluting or confusing them.
- **Is the trend sustainable?** Some trends are short-lived, while others are more adaptable. Choose trends that you can modify and make

your own rather than those that may feel dated soon.

## Tips for Incorporating Trends While Maintaining Brand Identity

Incorporating trends can bring a fresh look to your brand without straying too far from your core identity. Here's how to do it:

1. **Adapt Trends to Your Brand Colors**: If muted color palettes are trending, consider using your brand's color palette in muted tones to stay on-trend without losing your brand's recognizable hues.
2. **Customize Trendy Elements**: Add a unique twist to a popular trend. For example, if bold typography is in, use a distinctive font that reflects your brand's personality.
3. **Blend Trends with Existing Visual Styles**: Rather than a complete overhaul, integrate trending elements into your current style. For instance, adding motion graphics to an existing branded layout can bring it to life without changing the overall look.
4. **Experiment with A/B Testing**: Test trending visuals alongside traditional graphics to see

what resonates with your audience. A/B testing can help determine whether a trend is worth incorporating permanently.

5. **Embrace Trends Gradually**: Introduce trends slowly to avoid overwhelming your audience. Start by incorporating subtle elements of a trend, then gauge your audience's response before fully committing.

## Case Studies: Brands Successfully Leveraging Trends

Looking at examples of brands that have successfully adopted trends can offer inspiration. Here are a couple of brands that creatively leveraged trends without compromising their identity:

- **Airbnb**: Airbnb often incorporates minimalist aesthetics, muted colors, and candid photography to communicate a sense of comfort and warmth. Their visuals are trendy yet closely aligned with their brand's mission to create welcoming experiences.
- **Glossier**: Glossier uses pastel color palettes, bold typography, and authentic user-generated content to create a modern, approachable look. This trendy, minimalist approach reinforces

Glossier's emphasis on real beauty and relatability.

By analyzing these examples, you can see how brands stay relevant by thoughtfully adapting trends that enhance, rather than disrupt, their identity.

## Summary

Leveraging trends in social media graphics helps your brand stay relevant, engaging, and visually appealing. By choosing trends that align with your brand, testing their impact, and adapting them creatively, you can keep your visuals fresh without losing sight of your core identity. In the next chapter, we'll explore how to optimize your visuals for mobile to reach the growing number of mobile-first users.

# Chapter 9: Mobile Optimization of Visuals

With the majority of web traffic now coming from mobile devices, ensuring your visuals look great on small screens is essential. Mobile optimization isn't just about resizing images – it involves designing with mobile users in mind to ensure a seamless, engaging experience. In this chapter, we'll explore the importance of mobile optimization, practical strategies for adapting visuals to mobile, and tools for testing and refining your designs.

## Why Mobile Optimization Matters

Mobile users often have different expectations and behaviors compared to desktop users. They're typically looking for quick, easy access to information, with minimal effort required to navigate and view content. An image that looks fantastic on a desktop might appear cluttered or hard to read on a smaller screen. If your visuals aren't optimized for mobile, you risk losing engagement, frustrating users, and missing out on a significant portion of your audience.

**Benefits of mobile optimization include:**

- **Enhanced User Experience**: Mobile-friendly visuals make it easy for users to view and interact with content, improving overall satisfaction and engagement.
- **Better SEO Performance**: Search engines prioritize mobile-friendly websites in search results, so optimizing visuals for mobile can improve your visibility.
- **Increased Conversions**: Mobile-optimized visuals make it simpler for users to engage with calls-to-action, whether it's making a purchase, signing up, or sharing content.

## Key Considerations for Mobile-Optimized Visuals

1. **Size and Scale**
    - **Why It's Important**: Images that are too large or improperly scaled can slow down load times on mobile devices. Additionally, text within images should remain readable without requiring users to zoom in.
    - **Best Practice**: Resize images to fit mobile dimensions and avoid overly detailed visuals that can appear cluttered. Aim for dimensions of around

**640 to 1080 pixels** in width for typical mobile screens.

2. **File Format and Compression**
    - **Why It's Important**: Large files slow down loading times, especially for users on slower mobile connections.
    - **Best Practice**: Use compressed file formats like JPEG or WebP for images and MP4 for short video clips. Compress images to minimize file size while preserving quality.
3. **Responsive Layouts**
    - **Why It's Important**: Responsive layouts adjust automatically to fit any screen size, ensuring that images display properly on different devices.
    - **Best Practice**: Use responsive design techniques such as CSS media queries to resize and reposition images based on the screen size. For example, larger hero images on desktop can be replaced with smaller, cropped images on mobile.
4. **Readable Text**
    - **Why It's Important**: Small, intricate fonts may be hard to read on a mobile screen. Text within images should be large, clear, and easy to read.

- **Best Practice**: Use larger, bold fonts with high contrast against the background. Limit text to a few words or short phrases to avoid clutter. Test readability on different devices to ensure the text is accessible.

5. **Touch-Friendly CTAs**
   - **Why It's Important**: CTAs on mobile need to be easy to tap without accidentally hitting other elements. Buttons that are too small or too close together can frustrate users.
   - **Best Practice**: Design CTAs with ample padding and size them to be touch-friendly (recommended minimum size of 44x44 pixels). Ensure that clickable areas are spaced apart to prevent mis-taps.

## Practical Strategies for Mobile-Optimized Visuals

To create visuals that perform well on mobile, consider these specific strategies:

1. **Use Adaptive Images**

    - Adaptive images automatically adjust to different screen sizes and resolutions, reducing load times without sacrificing quality. Use the HTML srcset attribute to provide multiple image resolutions, allowing the browser to select the best option based on the user's device.
    - **Example**: Upload multiple versions of a product image at 320, 640, and 1080 pixels wide, and let the browser choose the appropriate size for each device.
2. **Minimize Text in Images**
    - Instead of embedding extensive text within images, overlay short, impactful phrases or CTAs. This allows the design to stay clean and the text to be readable.
    - **Example**: For a social media ad, use a short phrase like "Summer Sale – Shop Now!" instead of a detailed message, and include any additional information in the caption or post text.
3. **Focus on Central Elements**
    - Crop images to center on the most important elements. This makes the visual effective even on a smaller screen, without distracting background elements.

- **Example**: For a mobile product image, crop in closely on the product itself rather than including unnecessary background space, which might be more suitable for a desktop layout.

4. **Create Mobile-Friendly Infographics**
   - Traditional infographics may be too large or detailed for mobile screens. Break down complex infographics into multiple slides or carousel images that users can swipe through.
   - **Example**: Instead of one long infographic on "Top 10 Tips for Productivity," create a 10-image carousel with one tip per image.
5. **Use Video Thumbnails Strategically**
   - Videos autoplay on many social media platforms, but using a strong video thumbnail is still crucial for catching attention. For mobile, choose a thumbnail with bold visuals and minimal text.
   - **Example**: Use a close-up or action shot as the video thumbnail to capture attention immediately, ensuring users are more likely to engage.

## Testing Mobile Optimization

Once you've optimized your visuals for mobile, it's important to test them across various devices and screen sizes. Here are some tools and methods to help:

1. **Google Mobile-Friendly Test**
    - This free tool analyzes your website to determine if it's mobile-friendly and offers suggestions for improvements, such as adjusting image sizes or layout elements.
2. **Browser Developer Tools**
    - Most browsers, including Chrome and Firefox, have built-in developer tools that allow you to view your website on different device simulators. You can test how visuals look on popular screen sizes and orientations.
3. **Responsive Design Testing Tools**
    - Tools like **BrowserStack** and **Responsinator** allow you to preview how your images and layouts appear on a range of devices and operating systems, including Android, iOS, and desktop.

4. **Real Device Testing**
   - The most accurate test is to view your content on a variety of physical devices. Test visuals on both iOS and Android smartphones, tablets, and different screen sizes to ensure a consistent experience.

By testing thoroughly, you can catch any mobile optimization issues before they impact your audience, ensuring that your visuals look polished and professional on all screens.

## Mobile-Specific Considerations for Social Media Platforms

Social media platforms often prioritize mobile optimization by default, but certain best practices can help maximize engagement on these channels:

1. **Instagram and Facebook Stories**
   - Stories are viewed vertically on mobile, so design them to fit the **9:16 aspect ratio** (1080x1920 pixels). Use large text and high-contrast colors to ensure readability.
   - **Example**: Create eye-catching Story graphics with concise messages, vibrant

backgrounds, and a CTA like "Swipe up" for links.

2. **Pinterest Pins**
   - Pinterest recommends a **2:3 aspect ratio** for pins, such as 1000x1500 pixels. Vertical images perform better on mobile, where the Pinterest feed is designed for scrolling.
   - **Example**: For a recipe pin, use a vertical layout with a close-up image, a short recipe title, and a call-to-action like "Get the Recipe."
3. **YouTube Thumbnails**
   - YouTube thumbnails are often viewed on mobile devices, so design thumbnails with large, bold text and visually clear elements. Aim for an **aspect ratio of 16:9** (1280x720 pixels) and test on mobile to ensure legibility.
   - **Example**: Use high-contrast colors, close-up faces, and large fonts on YouTube thumbnails to make them stand out in mobile search results.
4. **Twitter Images**
   - Twitter's mobile interface crops images to fit within the feed, so use **16:9 aspect**

**ratio** (1200x675 pixels) and place key elements in the center.

  - **Example**: For a product announcement, position the product in the center of the image with concise text above or below it.

## Summary

Optimizing visuals for mobile devices is no longer optional; it's essential to reach and engage today's mobile-first audience. By resizing images, minimizing text, focusing on central elements, and testing across devices, you ensure a consistent, enjoyable experience for all users. Mobile optimization not only improves user satisfaction but also boosts your brand's credibility, SEO, and conversion potential.

In the next chapter, we'll explore measuring graphic performance to help you understand which visuals resonate most with your audience and drive results.

# Chapter 10: Measuring Graphic Performance – Analyzing What Works

Creating beautiful, engaging visuals is essential, but it's only half the battle. To make sure your graphics are truly effective, you need to measure their performance and analyze what resonates with your audience. This data-driven approach helps you refine your designs over time, maximizing their impact and supporting your brand goals.

In this chapter, we'll cover key metrics for measuring graphic performance, tools for tracking and analyzing results, and strategies for improving visuals based on audience insights.

## Why Measuring Graphic Performance Matters

Understanding the performance of your visuals allows you to make informed decisions that go beyond guesswork. By analyzing which images drive the most engagement, you can:

- **Boost Engagement**: Identify the elements that capture attention and encourage interaction, leading to higher likes, shares, and comments.
- **Enhance Conversion Rates**: Determine which visuals are most effective at driving conversions, helping you improve your return on investment.
- **Refine Your Brand Strategy**: Gain insights into your audience's preferences, allowing you to align your visuals more closely with their needs and interests.

With the right data, you can make tweaks that maximize the impact of every visual, improving overall effectiveness and supporting your brand's goals.

## Key Metrics for Measuring Graphic Performance

Tracking the right metrics is essential to understanding how well your visuals are performing.

Here are some of the most important metrics to consider:

1. **Engagement Rate**
    - **What It Is**: Engagement rate measures the number of interactions (likes, comments, shares) relative to the total reach or impressions. It indicates how compelling your visuals are to viewers.
    - **Why It Matters**: A high engagement rate shows that your content resonates with your audience and encourages interaction.
    - **How to Track It**: Platforms like Instagram and Facebook provide engagement rates in their insights sections. Alternatively, you can calculate it manually as (total engagements / total impressions) * 100.
2. **Click-Through Rate (CTR)**
    - **What It Is**: CTR is the percentage of users who click on a link or call-to-action (CTA) within your visual.
    - **Why It Matters**: CTR reveals how effectively your visuals drive users to take action, such as visiting your website or making a purchase.
    - **How to Track It**: For website graphics, use tools like Google Analytics to measure CTR on image links. Social

platforms also track CTR for ads and posts with clickable elements.

3. **Conversion Rate**
    - **What It Is**: Conversion rate is the percentage of users who complete a desired action (such as signing up, downloading, or purchasing) after interacting with your visual.
    - **Why It Matters**: This metric shows how well your visuals contribute to achieving business goals, such as generating leads or sales.
    - **How to Track It**: For website graphics, track conversion rate through Google Analytics. Many social media ads platforms also measure conversions for paid campaigns.
4. **Impressions and Reach**
    - **What It Is**: Impressions are the total number of times your visual was displayed, while reach refers to the number of unique viewers.
    - **Why It Matters**: These metrics help you understand how widely your content is being seen and how effectively it reaches your target audience.

    - **How to Track It**: Impressions and reach are tracked by most social media platforms and analytics tools, including Facebook Insights, Instagram Insights, and Twitter Analytics.
5. **Save and Share Rate**
    - **What It Is**: Save and share rate measures how often users save your visuals to revisit later or share them with others.
    - **Why It Matters**: A high save or share rate indicates that your content provides value and is likely to have a lasting impact.
    - **How to Track It**: Platforms like Instagram provide save and share data in their insights. On other platforms, track shares and downloads to measure user interest.
6. **Scroll Depth (for Web Pages)**
    - **What It Is**: Scroll depth measures how far users scroll on a page. For visuals placed within web pages, it shows whether users are engaging with the content.
    - **Why It Matters**: Scroll depth data can help you understand if users are

reaching and viewing your visuals, especially on longer pages.

- **How to Track It**: Use Google Analytics or plugins to track scroll depth on pages with important visuals.

## Tools for Tracking and Analyzing Visual Performance

Various tools are available to help you measure graphic performance and analyze results. Here are some popular options:

1. **Google Analytics**
   - **What It Does**: Google Analytics tracks user interactions on your website, including CTR, conversions, and scroll depth.
   - **Best For**: Website visuals, banners, and images with links to track visitor behavior.
   - **Tips**: Set up goals in Google Analytics to track specific conversions related to visuals, like downloads or product clicks.

2. **Social Media Analytics**
    - **What It Does**: Each major social platform (Facebook, Instagram, Twitter, LinkedIn, Pinterest) provides insights on engagement, reach, CTR, and more.
    - **Best For**: Social media posts, ads, and stories.
    - **Tips**: Use these insights to compare performance across different visuals and identify what works best on each platform.
3. **Heatmap Tools (e.g., Hotjar, Crazy Egg)**
    - **What It Does**: Heatmaps show where users click, scroll, and linger on a webpage, revealing how they interact with images and CTAs.
    - **Best For**: Landing pages, product pages, and any visual-heavy web page.
    - **Tips**: Use heatmaps to see if users are engaging with visuals as intended and if they're drawn to key CTAs.

4. **A/B Testing Platforms (e.g., Optimizely, VWO)**
    - **What It Does**: A/B testing tools allow you to test different versions of visuals to see which performs better.
    - **Best For**: Testing the effectiveness of design elements like colors, text, and layout in ads, web banners, and landing pages.
    - **Tips**: Run A/B tests for individual elements (e.g., CTA color or headline) to isolate what drives the best performance.

## Using Data to Optimize Visuals

Once you've gathered performance data, the next step is to apply those insights to optimize your visuals. Here are some strategies based on common data findings:

1. **Improve Visual Hierarchy Based on Click and Heatmap Data**
    - **Finding**: Users may be clicking on elements that aren't primary CTAs or ignoring important visuals.

- **Solution**: Redesign to establish a clear visual hierarchy, drawing attention to key CTAs or important messages through contrasting colors, bold text, or strategic placement.

2. **Refine CTAs Using A/B Testing Results**
    - **Finding**: One version of a CTA button gets significantly more clicks than another.
    - **Solution**: Use the winning CTA design across similar visuals. Experiment with variations in wording, color, and placement to further optimize.
3. **Adjust Image Style Based on Engagement Rates**
    - **Finding**: Authentic, candid photos have higher engagement rates than polished, staged images.
    - **Solution**: Incorporate more authentic visuals in your content strategy, especially on social media, where users prefer relatable imagery.
4. **Optimize for Mobile if Scroll Depth is Low**
    - **Finding**: Users aren't scrolling far enough to view your visuals, especially on mobile.

    - **Solution**: Reposition important visuals higher on the page and ensure they're mobile-optimized. Consider testing different image formats or aspect ratios that work better on small screens.
5. **Increase Readability with Text Overlays**
    - **Finding**: Heatmaps show users spending little time on graphics with heavy text.
    - **Solution**: Simplify text in images, focusing on concise, impactful phrases. Increase contrast and font size to ensure readability on smaller screens.

## Creating a Visual Performance Dashboard

To keep track of your metrics over time, consider setting up a performance dashboard. This can be a simple spreadsheet or a dashboard in analytics software, allowing you to track metrics like engagement rate, CTR, conversion rate, and impressions. A performance dashboard helps you spot trends, benchmark visuals, and quickly identify which content types are driving results.

## Summary

Measuring the performance of your visuals is essential to understand what resonates with your audience and drives results. By tracking key metrics like engagement rate, CTR, and conversions, and using tools like Google Analytics and heatmaps, you can gain valuable insights into your audience's preferences. With this data, you can optimize your visuals to maximize their impact, making each design decision smarter and more strategic.

In the next chapter, we'll wrap up with a resource directory of tools and sites for creating, editing, and optimizing graphics to support your visual content journey.

# Chapter 11: AI Tools for Visual Creation – The Future of Graphic Design

Artificial Intelligence (AI) is transforming the way we create visuals, offering tools that are faster, smarter, and more accessible than ever. With AI, you can generate professional-quality graphics, automate tedious tasks, and even brainstorm creative ideas—all without the need for advanced design skills. This chapter explores the opportunities and challenges of using AI tools for visual creation, providing a practical guide to integrating AI into your design workflow.

## The Rise of AI in Graphic Design

AI-powered design tools have become increasingly popular in recent years, and for good reason. These tools use machine learning algorithms to analyze patterns, predict trends, and create visuals that resonate with your audience. What once required hours of manual effort can now be done in minutes, making AI a game-changer for businesses, marketers, and content creators.

Whether you're a seasoned designer or a beginner, AI tools can enhance your creative process by:

- Saving Time: Automating repetitive tasks like resizing, cropping, or creating variations of a design.
- Enhancing Creativity: Offering design suggestions, generating ideas, and exploring new styles.
- Improving Accessibility: Making high-quality design accessible to non-designers through intuitive interfaces.

## Popular AI Tools for Visual Creation

Here are some of the most popular AI tools transforming the graphic design landscape:

1. **Canva AI**
    - What It Does: Canva AI offers automated design suggestions, generates text-to-image graphics, and simplifies complex design tasks with drag-and-drop ease.
    - Best Features:
        - Magic Resize: Instantly adjust designs to fit various social media formats.

        - Text-to-Image: Generate unique visuals from a written prompt.
        - Style Suggestions: AI-based layout and font recommendations.
    - Why It's Useful: Canva AI makes professional-quality design accessible, especially for those with little to no design experience.

2. **Adobe Sensei**
    - What It Does: Adobe Sensei powers AI features across Adobe Creative Cloud, automating tasks like background removal, font pairing, and photo editing.
    - Best Features:
        - Content-Aware Fill: Automatically remove unwanted elements from images.
        - Auto Reframe: Adjust video aspect ratios for different platforms.
        - Pattern Generation: Create complex patterns with minimal effort.
    - Why It's Useful: For experienced designers, Adobe Sensei speeds up

workflows without compromising creative control.

3. **DALL·E**
   - What It Does: DALL·E is an AI model that generates images from textual descriptions, offering endless creative possibilities.
   - Best Features:
     - Text-to-Image: Create completely unique visuals by describing what you want.
     - Variations: Generate different versions of an image based on your input.
     - Edits: Make changes to existing images using natural language prompts.
   - Why It's Useful: DALL·E enables users to create highly customized visuals that would be difficult or time-consuming to produce manually.
4. **MidJourney: AI for Stunning, Artistic Visuals**
   - What It Does: MidJourney is an AI-powered tool that focuses on generating highly artistic and

imaginative visuals from text prompts. Known for its unique, creative outputs, MidJourney is particularly popular among artists, designers, and marketers looking to add a distinct, eye-catching aesthetic to their projects.

- Best Features:
    - Text-to-Image Generation: Create intricate, artistic visuals by simply describing what you want.
    - Style Customization: Adjust the artistic style of your output, from photo realistic to abstract or painterly.
    - High Resolution: Generate visuals with exceptional detail and clarity, suitable for both digital and print.
- Why It's Useful: MidJourney excels in creating unique, high-quality visuals that stand out. It's ideal for branding projects, mood boards, and marketing campaigns where originality is key. Unlike more utilitarian AI tools, MidJourney's strength lies in its ability

to deliver visually stunning, almost ethereal designs.

- Example Use Cases:
- Brand Identity: Generate artistic backgrounds or conceptual visuals that reflect your brand's personality.
- Social Media Content: Create scroll-stopping, artistic posts to enhance engagement.
- Creative Exploration: Experiment with visual styles and concepts for inspiration or brainstorming.

## 5. Runway ML

- What It Does: Runway ML focuses on AI-powered video and visual editing, including background removal and text-to-video generation.
- Best Features:
  - Green Screen: Remove or replace backgrounds in videos with AI precision.
  - Text-to-Video: Create short videos from written descriptions.
  - Style Transfer: Apply unique artistic styles to images or videos.

- Why It's Useful: Runway ML is ideal for creators looking to integrate AI into video-heavy projects.

## Pros and Cons of Using AI-Generated Visuals

Like any tool, AI-powered design tools come with both benefits and limitations. Here's a balanced look at what AI can (and can't) do:

**Pros:**

- Efficiency: AI dramatically reduces the time spent on repetitive tasks, freeing up your creativity for more complex projects.
- Accessibility: Non-designers can create polished visuals without needing extensive training.
- Cost-Effectiveness: Many AI tools are affordable or offer free versions, reducing the need for expensive design software or professional services.
- Endless Possibilities: AI can generate ideas or visuals that you might not have thought of, expanding your creative potential.

**Cons:**

- Lack of Originality: AI-generated visuals can sometimes lack the unique touch of a human designer, leading to content that feels generic or repetitive.
- Learning Curve: While many tools are user-friendly, understanding how to get the best results from AI requires experimentation and practice.
- Ethical Concerns: The use of AI in design raises questions about intellectual property, copyright, and the potential for misuse (e.g., deepfakes).

## Ethical Considerations in AI Design

As AI becomes more prevalent in design, it's important to consider the ethical implications. Here are some key issues to keep in mind:

1. **Copyright and Ownership**
    - AI-generated visuals often come with unclear copyright terms. Who owns the image—the user who inputs the prompt or the company that built the AI? Always check the licensing terms of the tool you're using.

2. **Plagiarism Risks**
   - AI models are trained on vast datasets, which can include copyrighted material. This raises concerns about whether the generated visuals inadvertently replicate existing works.
3. **Transparency**
   - If you're using AI-generated visuals for commercial purposes, be transparent about the process. Customers may appreciate knowing how your visuals were created.
4. **Misuse**
   - Ensure your use of AI respects ethical guidelines. Avoid using the technology for misleading or harmful purposes, such as creating fake endorsements or misleading imagery.

## Best Practices for Integrating AI into Your Workflow

1. **Combine AI with Human Creativity**
   - Use AI as a starting point, not a replacement. Combine AI-generated

elements with your unique creative touch to produce visuals that stand out.

2. **Experiment and Iterate**
   - AI tools improve with input. Don't be afraid to experiment with different prompts, settings, or features to refine your results.
3. **Understand the Limitations**
   - Know when AI is the right tool and when a professional designer or manual work might be more appropriate. For example, highly detailed branding projects may still require a human touch.
4. **Stay Updated**
   - AI tools are constantly evolving. Keep an eye on updates, new features, and emerging platforms to stay ahead of the curve.

## The Future of AI in Design

AI is reshaping the design landscape, making it more accessible, efficient, and innovative. While it won't replace human creativity, it's a powerful tool for amplifying your efforts and unlocking new possibilities. As AI continues to evolve, staying informed and ethical in its use will help you harness its full potential.

## Summary

AI-powered tools like Canva AI, Adobe Sensei, DALL·E, and MidJourney are revolutionizing graphic design, offering faster workflows, endless creative possibilities, and the ability to produce highly artistic and unique visuals. While these tools provide significant advantages, understanding their limitations and ethical implications is essential for using them responsibly. By integrating AI into your design process, you can create impactful visuals with greater ease and efficiency, setting your brand apart in a competitive digital landscape.

# Chapter 12: Resource Directory – Tools and Sites for Creating High-Quality Graphics

Creating high-quality graphics is easier when you have the right tools and resources at your fingertips. From graphic design software and stock photo websites to image compression tools and accessibility checkers, this chapter provides a curated list of resources that can help you produce visually stunning, effective graphics.

## Graphic Design Software and Tools

Whether you're creating social media posts, infographics, or website banners, graphic design software is the foundation of any visual content strategy. Here are some of the top design tools for creating high-quality graphics:

1. **Adobe Photoshop**
    - **Best For**: Advanced photo editing, graphic design, and detailed visuals.

    - **Features**: Layers, filters, brushes, and extensive editing tools.
    - **Pricing**: Subscription-based, with various plans through Adobe Creative Cloud.
    - **Why It's Great**: Photoshop offers powerful tools for detailed editing and customization, making it ideal for professional-grade designs.
2. **Canva**
    - **Best For**: Easy-to-use graphic design for beginners and non-designers.
    - **Features**: Drag-and-drop interface, customizable templates, text overlays, and stock images.
    - **Pricing**: Free version with optional Pro subscription for additional features.
    - **Why It's Great**: Canva provides an extensive library of templates, making it perfect for quick social media posts, presentations, and marketing materials.
3. **Adobe Illustrator**
    - **Best For**: Vector graphics, logos, and illustrations.
    - **Features**: Advanced vector tools, typography customization, and scalable graphics.

- **Pricing**: Subscription-based, available through Adobe Creative Cloud.
- **Why It's Great**: Illustrator is ideal for creating scalable graphics, like logos and icons, without sacrificing quality.

4. **Figma**
   - **Best For**: Collaborative design, especially for UI/UX and web graphics.
   - **Features**: Real-time collaboration, prototyping, and responsive design tools.
   - **Pricing**: Free version available; premium plans for additional features.
   - **Why It's Great**: Figma's collaborative features make it perfect for teams working together on visual projects.
5. **GIMP (GNU Image Manipulation Program)**
   - **Best For**: Free, open-source alternative to Photoshop.
   - **Features**: Layered editing, filters, brushes, and customizable interface.
   - **Pricing**: Free.
   - **Why It's Great**: GIMP is powerful and flexible, offering many of the same features as Photoshop without the subscription cost.

## Stock Photos and Image Resources

Quality images can elevate your content and make it more engaging. Here are some top sites for sourcing high-quality stock photos, illustrations, and videos:

1. **Unsplash**
   - **Best For**: Free, high-quality stock photography.
   - **Features**: Extensive library of free-to-use images with no attribution required.
   - **Pricing**: Free.
   - **Why It's Great**: Unsplash offers a wide selection of beautiful, high-resolution images that are free for personal and commercial use.
2. **Shutterstock**
   - **Best For**: Premium stock photos, vectors, and videos.
   - **Features**: Large library of royalty-free images, videos, and music, with various licensing options.
   - **Pricing**: Subscription or pay-per-image plans.
   - **Why It's Great**: Shutterstock provides diverse and high-quality content,

including niche categories and professional images.

3. **Pexels**
    - **Best For**: Free stock photography and video clips.
    - **Features**: Free-to-use photos and videos with no attribution required, searchable by categories and tags.
    - **Pricing**: Free.
    - **Why It's Great**: Pexels offers an extensive library of stock photos and videos that are perfect for social media, blogs, and website visuals.
4. **Adobe Stock**
    - **Best For**: High-quality, premium stock images and illustrations.
    - **Features**: Integrated with Adobe Creative Cloud, providing access to stock photos directly in Adobe apps.
    - **Pricing**: Subscription or pay-per-image plans.
    - **Why It's Great**: Adobe Stock integrates seamlessly with Photoshop and Illustrator, making it easy to incorporate high-quality images into your design workflow.
5. **Pixabay**

- **Best For**: Free stock photos, illustrations, vectors, and videos.
- **Features**: Free for personal and commercial use, with images in various categories and styles.
- **Pricing**: Free.
- **Why It's Great**: Pixabay offers a large library of free resources, from photos and illustrations to vector graphics, with simple licensing for worry-free use.

## Image Optimization and Compression Tools

Optimizing images for web and mobile ensures fast loading times without compromising quality. These tools can help you compress and optimize images for different platforms:

1. **TinyPNG / TinyJPG**
    - **Best For**: Compressing PNG and JPEG images for faster web performance.
    - **Features**: Simple, drag-and-drop interface with high compression rates.
    - **Pricing**: Free for basic use; paid plans for additional features.

- **Why It's Great**: TinyPNG and TinyJPG reduce file sizes without noticeable quality loss, making them ideal for optimizing images for websites.

2. **ImageOptim**
   - **Best For**: Lossless compression for multiple image formats.
   - **Features**: Optimizes PNG, JPEG, and GIF files by removing metadata and compressing files.
   - **Pricing**: Free (Mac only).
   - **Why It's Great**: ImageOptim is a powerful, no-cost tool for macOS users, delivering effective compression without quality loss.
3. **Squoosh (by Google)**
   - **Best For**: Web-based image compression with multiple format options.
   - **Features**: Supports various file formats and lets you adjust quality settings in real-time.
   - **Pricing**: Free.
   - **Why It's Great**: Squoosh is flexible and easy to use, allowing users to experiment with different compression

levels to find the right balance of quality and file size.

4. **JPEG-Optimizer**
   - **Best For**: Simple online JPEG compression.
   - **Features**: Adjusts JPEG quality and resizing for faster web performance.
   - **Pricing**: Free.
   - **Why It's Great**: JPEG-Optimizer is straightforward and effective, especially for basic JPEG compression needs.

## Accessibility Tools

To ensure that your visuals are accessible to all users, these tools help you test and adjust for readability, contrast, and compliance with accessibility standards:

1. **WAVE (Web Accessibility Evaluation Tool)**
   - **Best For**: Checking web pages for accessibility, including alt text and color contrast.
   - **Features**: Identifies accessibility issues, with suggestions for improvements.
   - **Pricing**: Free.
   - **Why It's Great**: WAVE is easy to use and provides an in-depth report, making

it simple to spot and fix accessibility issues.

2. **Color Contrast Checker (by WebAIM)**
    - **Best For**: Ensuring text within images meets color contrast guidelines.
    - **Features**: Allows you to test color combinations to meet WCAG standards.
    - **Pricing**: Free.
    - **Why It's Great**: This tool helps you confirm that text within images is readable for users with visual impairments, improving accessibility.
3. **axe Accessibility Checker**
    - **Best For**: Comprehensive accessibility testing for web content.
    - **Features**: Browser extension for testing color contrast, alt text, and other accessibility features.
    - **Pricing**: Free.
    - **Why It's Great**: axe Accessibility Checker provides thorough accessibility testing directly within your browser.

## Collaboration and Project Management Tools

When working with teams, having a reliable project management tool can streamline the design process and keep everyone aligned. Here are a few popular tools for design collaboration:

1. **Trello**
    - **Best For**: Visual project management and task tracking.
    - **Features**: Kanban-style boards, checklists, and team collaboration.
    - **Pricing**: Free plan with optional paid upgrades.
    - **Why It's Great**: Trello's visual interface makes it easy to track design progress and share updates with team members.
2. **Asana**
    - **Best For**: Task management and team collaboration on complex projects.
    - **Features**: Project timelines, task assignments, and progress tracking.
    - **Pricing**: Free version available; premium plans for more features.
    - **Why It's Great**: Asana's project management tools help keep design

tasks organized and ensure that deadlines are met.

3. **Slack**
    - **Best For**: Team communication and file sharing.
    - **Features**: Channels for team discussions, direct messaging, and integrations with design tools.
    - **Pricing**: Free version available; paid plans for additional features.
    - **Why It's Great**: Slack enables quick communication and file sharing, making it easier to collaborate and get feedback on design work.

## Summary

This resource directory provides you with the essential tools and sites to create, optimize, and manage high-quality graphics. With options for all skill levels and budgets, these resources empower you to produce professional visuals that resonate with your audience and enhance your brand's online presence.

# Chapter 13: Bringing It All Together – A Roadmap for Visual Success

You've learned the foundational principles, tools, and techniques for creating engaging, effective, and brand-aligned visuals. In this final chapter, we'll recap the key takeaways and provide actionable steps to implement what you've learned, helping you turn your visual content strategy into a powerful tool for brand growth and engagement.

## Key Takeaways from Each Chapter

1. **Understanding File Types**
   Choose the right file type based on the needs of your visual, balancing quality with performance. JPEG, PNG, SVG, and WebP all serve unique roles in your design toolkit.
2. **Optimizing File Sizes and Load Times**
   Compress images and adjust file sizes to reduce load times and improve user experience, especially for mobile users and SEO.
3. **Using the Right Dimensions for Each Platform**

Tailor your image dimensions to fit each platform's guidelines, ensuring your visuals appear polished and professional wherever they're shared.

4. **Maintaining Brand Consistency**
   A cohesive visual style builds trust and recognition. Use a style guide to keep colors, fonts, and imagery aligned with your brand identity.
5. **Navigating Copyright and Licensing**
   Protect your brand by using licensed images responsibly, and understand the importance of proper attribution and copyright compliance.
6. **Making Images Accessible**
   Ensure all users can engage with your visuals by following accessibility guidelines, using alt text, and optimizing for contrast and readability.
7. **Creating Engagement-Driven Graphics**
   Design visuals that encourage interaction by focusing on emotional appeal, clear CTAs, and visual hierarchy to draw users in.
8. **Leveraging Trends in Social Media Graphics**
   Stay relevant by incorporating current visual trends while staying true to your brand's core identity. Test what works and adjust based on engagement.

9. **Optimizing for Mobile**
   Design with mobile-first principles, making sure that visuals are easily viewable and engaging on smaller screens.
10. **Measuring Graphic Performance**
    Use metrics like engagement rate, CTR, and conversions to gauge what works, refining your strategy to maximize impact.
11. **Using the Right Tools and Resources**
    Equip yourself with the right tools for design, image optimization, and accessibility testing to streamline your workflow and enhance graphic quality.

## Building a Sustainable Visual Strategy

Creating a sustainable visual strategy means staying adaptable and continually refining your approach. Here are some tips for maintaining momentum:

- **Regularly Update Your Style Guide**: Revisit your style guide as your brand evolves, making adjustments to colors, fonts, or visual elements as needed.
- **Stay Informed on Trends**: Visual trends change quickly. Check in periodically to see if

new styles align with your brand or audience, experimenting where it makes sense.

- **Engage in A/B Testing**: Regularly test different visuals to understand what resonates with your audience. Data-driven adjustments keep your visuals relevant and engaging.
- **Review Performance Metrics Consistently**: Set aside time each month or quarter to review visual performance metrics. Analyze what works and identify areas for improvement.

## Final Thoughts

Effective visuals are more than just aesthetics; they are a strategic tool for connecting with your audience, building trust, and achieving your brand goals. With the right knowledge, tools, and an adaptive approach, your visuals can become a powerful force that drives engagement, elevates your brand, and enhances your online presence.

By implementing the techniques and strategies covered in this book, you'll be equipped to create compelling, high-quality visuals that leave a lasting impression.

Thank you for joining me on this journey. Here's to creating visuals that not only look great but also work hard for your brand.

# Epilogue: The Next Step in Your Journey

Congratulations! By diving into the principles, tools, and strategies in *Visual Impact: The Ultimate Guide to Website and Social Media Graphics*, you've equipped yourself with the knowledge to create visuals that truly make a difference. You now understand how to design graphics that not only look great but also enhance your brand, engage your audience, and drive results.

But your journey doesn't have to stop here.

If you're ready to take your website to the next level, I invite you to explore my book *Unlocking Website Profits*. This guide is packed with actionable strategies to help you transform your website into a powerful tool for generating leads, driving sales, and growing your business. You can find it on Amazon or by visiting **frankdeardurff.com**, where you'll also discover a variety of services designed to support entrepreneurs and small business owners like you.

Whether you're looking to optimize your website, craft a winning digital strategy, or create a standout online presence, I'm here to help. Visit

**frankdeardurff.com** to learn more about how we can work together to achieve your goals.

Thank you for allowing me to be part of your journey. Keep creating, keep growing, and remember: impactful visuals can change everything.

Here's to your continued success,
Frank E. Deardurff III
That One Web Guy

Made in the USA
Monee, IL
04 November 2026

67376802R00079